PRA'

CW01500309

O sing
for God has done marvelous things.
Make a joyful noise to
the Lord, all the earth;
break forth into joyous song
and sing praises.

(Psalm 98:1, 4)

Go tell it on
the mountain
that Jesus
Christ is born.

I must confess — I am
a Christmas Christian.
While all the holy days of
Christianity, and most partic-
ularly Good Friday and Easter,
are connected, and all define my

spirituality, the birth of Jesus in its wonder and simplicity is at the heart of my faith. Perhaps this is because I am a father and a grandfather. I witnessed and coached our son's birth and beheld my grandsons a few hours after they were born. Nothing is more common and yet more wonderful than the birth of a child. According to some estimates, in the 300-thousand-year adventure of *homo sapiens*, nearly 120 billion babies have been born. In the birth of a child, and in your own birth, the universal meets the particular and the infinite joins the finite in the wonders of God's love. Like snowflakes, each birth is unique and unrepeatable, and with each birth, as Celtic spiritual guide Pelagius exclaimed, we see the face of God.

I am entranced by the images of Christmas: the star in the East, the magi on their camels, the awestruck shepherds overwhelmed by the angelic chorus, the humble stable, the holy infant, and the mother and father with their firstborn child. I am amazed by the miracles of Christmas: the angelic visitation to Mary, Joseph's dreams, and signs in the heavens. The Incarnation of God's Word and Wisdom gives light and hope to every weary traveler and propels the moral and spiritual arcs of history forward. The Infinite is in the finite. Divinity is in humanity, and humanity gives birth to Divinity. Thin places of spiritual transformation and beauty everywhere.

PRAYING TWICE

The 12 Days of Christmas with Carols and Hymns

PRAYING TWICE

The 12 Days of Christmas with Carols and Hymns

BRUCE G. EPPERLY

ANAMCHARA
BOOKS

Anamchara Books
Vestal, New York 13850
www.AnamcharaBooks.com

Paperback ISBN: 978-1-62524-871-8
eBook ISBN: 978-1-62524-850-3

CONTENTS

I resonate with Good Friday's portrait of God as "the fellow sufferer who understands" and Jesus' willingness to sacrifice for Creation's healing. I am amazed at Easter visions revealing the triumph of life over death, love over hate, and the resurrection releasing the healing presence of Jesus to renew our cells and souls. Still, it is Christmas that shapes my faith.

Without Christ's birth, there would be no ministry, prophetic word, cross, or empty tomb. While Good Friday and Easter are not afterthoughts, first comes Incarnation, the original blessing of God's creativity in birthing the universe, guiding the galaxies, shaping earthly evolution, and inspiring the better angels of our nature. As theologian and singer-songwriter Sheri Kling wrote:

God is embodied, Word become flesh, in all that we see.
Deeply incarnate in every bird, in every tree.
In the heartbeat of billions of bodies just wanting to be.
God is embodied, soul of the world, breathing in me.

All things have value, all the way up and all the way down.
God is redeeming the lowliest stone and the glorious crown.
Christ is the pattern in every atom around.
All things have value, whispering Spirit Sound.

Christmas carols and hymns, which I sing all year long, reveal to me the miracle and wonder of Jesus' birth, both in Bethlehem and with each new day. I begin playing Christmas carols in earnest on Thanksgiving weekend and continue through the Advent season. The twelve days of Christmas, from December 25 to January 5, are filled with "joy to the world" and "silent nights." On the Feast of Epiphany, I "tell it on the mountain that Jesus Christ is born." My hallelujahs are full-hearted as I sing along with Handel's "Messiah," walk before sunrise singing "O Come All Ye Faithful," or croon John Rutter's "Candlelight Carol" as I go about household chores. Filled with the spirit of Christmas, I have to remind myself not to disturb my wife or neighbors with my praise!

I once surprised a colleague when I asserted that "if all we had were the Christmas carols, and no scriptures, that would be enough for me to affirm God incarnate in Jesus of Nazareth." Listening to these old, familiar songs, I am captivated by the vision of God, among us and in my life. For a moment, I am no longer a seasoned theologian but a magus following the star and a shepherd serenaded by angels.

I realize that the process of divinizing Christ, seeing him as God incarnate, is a complicated and challenging story that evolved over centuries. "How Jesus became God," as New Testament scholar Bart Ehrman asserts, is important. But, more important to our spiritual growth than biblical scholarship, is the theological and spiritual affirmation that "the whole earth is full of God's glory" and that "the wonders of God's love" were fully manifest in Bethlehem's stable and in the life, ministry, death, and resurrection of Jesus of Nazareth—and that these events can transform our lives. In singing or listening to Christmas carols, we experience what Celtic spiritual guides call a "thin place," in this case, the thin place of God's revelation in a Child that awakens us to experience Divinity everywhere. "The true light, which enlightens everyone, was coming into the world" (John 1:9). We realize that beyond the factuality of the stories or the accuracy of our Christmas pageants, lies the deeper truth of the birth of God's child in the chaos and conflict of history, our own and our planet's.

Saint Augustine is reputed to have said that those who sing pray twice. In our Christmas carols, we find praise, contemplation, lamentation, and affirmation. When we sing, we join the angelic chorus with the shepherds and listen to the harmonies of the spheres that inspired the Greek philosopher Pythagoras and his followers. Like the author of Psalm 148, we claim our role as choristers in a world of praise. With Handel, we sing "Hallelujah" in the hope of the reign of God's love in the world.

Our Christmas carols rise to the heavens and plumb the unconscious depths of the Spirit, where the "sighs too deep for words" whisper. Childhood memories of carols linger at the edges of our memories even when we have difficulty remembering our names. More than once, while leading worship services at convalescent hospitals, residents of the memory care unit joined us, and immediately perked up and sang along to "Silent Night" and "O Little Town of Bethlehem." God's amazing grace still spoke to them in hymns of childhood that guided their lives. There is an Incarnation in each of us that memory can't erase.

I am not alone in my Christmas spirituality and delight in the carols. Church musician, composer, and former colleague at Lancaster Theological Seminary, Daryl Hollinger, describes the contours of his Christmas spirit: "Of all the seasons of the year, Christmas is it. I love the season and I love the carols. Perhaps, it's the nostalgia, the warm feelings of memories singing carols at church, caroling in the neighborhood and to shut-ins, the tree and the decorations, the baking and the eating."[1] Daryl continues with the affirmation that "Christmas is more than nostalgic memories of childhood." As a committed church musician, Daryl asserts that "the challenge is to deepen our spirituality during the Christmas season, and to recognize that singing the hymns moves us from heart to mind as we seek the meaning of Christmas for us now." In his role as choir director, Daryl often asks his choirs, "What are we singing in this music? What do the words mean to us?"

One of Daryl's favorite carols is "Silent Night." Viewing the congregation lighting candles and listening to the congregation's meditative singing, Daryl says, "I'm always moved. The words 'all is calm' remind me in the midst of the hustle and bustle and commercialization of Christmas, there is something more, something deeper to cherish and celebrate." As he rehearses and plays another favorite carol, "In the Bleak Midwinter," Daryl reflects that "while the hymn may not be historically accurate—there probably wasn't snow in Bethlehem—the words 'what can I give him? I give him my heart' always call me to reflect about what I will give Jesus."

Another of my colleagues, theologian, musician, and former student Sheri Kling[2] "vividly recalls going to the 11:00 p.m. Candlelight Service on Christmas Eve. As a child, staying up late to celebrate Jesus' birth was a special treat." Like Daryl, Sheri was moved by the "candles in the darkness." Then, and now, Sheri treasures childhood memories, and connects these with "the eternal now, the cloud of witnesses, gathered for worship, joining the whole body of Christ." Another strong memory for Sheri is making Advent wreaths at church potluck dinners and lighting candles at home. Christmas joins the "hopes and fears of all the years." It also revives memories, joining past and future, the living and the dead in one great hymn of wonder and praise.

During my years as a congregational pastor, my congregants came to expect that I would celebrate "Christmas in July" with the inclusion of carols such as "Joy to the World" and "O Come All Ye Faithful" in worship. In the chaos of our times, including services on Zoom during Covid season, we needed a sense of God's light piercing the darkness of the world: incivility and violence that threatened our national well-being; the fear and anxiety we felt as we watched hatred enacted in school shootings, military invasions, and violence against the LGBTQ community and asylum seekers; and our fears that we would be among the Covid casualties. We needed "a little Christmas," a sense that God was with us, just as God was present in the birth of a Child in humble circumstances under the violent rule of the Roman Empire. We didn't need abstract orthodoxy or hyper-intellectualized biblical scholarship; we needed to sing hymns of faith to help us experience the faithful intimacy of Emmanuel, God-with-Us, gathering up our "hopes and fears" and providing us courage for today and hope for the future.

BREATHING
YOUR FAITH

Let everything
that breathes,
praise God!
Praise God!

(Psalm 150:6)

B reath is the heart of life.
God creates by breathing
over the void, energizing the
universe's journey, and bringing forth the light of our world
(Genesis 1:1–3). That same
everlasting and ever-present Divine breath, revealed in God's
energy of love, breathes and inspires all Creation, giving birth
to a world of praise. On Easter night, the Risen Jesus blessed
his followers and us with the words, "Peace be with you. As
the Father has sent me, so I send you" and breathed on them

and said to them, "Receive the Holy Spirit" (John 20:21–22). When we breathe, we are inspired, and when we sing, we send our inspiration out into the universe. In song, we participate in God's holy breath, joining mind, body, spirit, and relationships, sending a joyful breath to the ambient world. We share the breath of Creation and resurrection as we bring joy to the world.

As health-care providers—including physicians, nurses, and holistic healers—note, breath calms and focuses. Breath energizes our spirits and awakens us to new energy. When we breathe deeply and let our breath flow, our singing range expands, and our songs project out into the world.

Of course, the world of the shepherds, magi, angels, and holy family is very different from our own. They traveled by foot and horse, while we journey by automobile, jet, and space shuttle. They communicated by voice and parchment; we communicate by digital imagery, social media, and electronic mail, as well as the spoken voice on phones and in person. Our carols are now local and global, whereas those long-ago hymns were personal and communal. Despite the differences, however, the Christmas carols, and the biblical stories on which they are based, still speak to anxiety and hope, even to our personal, political, and social situations today.

These songs calm, enliven, and enlighten. The angelic voices recorded in scripture as hymns, dreams, and visitations, along with Mary's Magnificat, shed the same light on the social and political worlds of both the first and twenty-first centuries. They call us beyond polarization and injustice to "peace on earth, goodwill to all."

Then, as now, Christmas is political as well as personal, and the carols call us to compassion for the stranger, immigrant, and marginalized. As the hymns proclaim, "the slave is our brother," and the bells peal, telling us that "God is not dead, nor doth God sleep, the wrong shall fail, the right prevail," and peace on Earth shall reign. That is our Christmas dream and the hope that inspires heart, head, and hands. We breathe deeply, receive the breath of God, and are empowered to calmly respond to the challenges of our personal, family, and political lives. Our souls—and all souls—"find their worth."

At Christmas, gathered for worship or listening to carols at home, we sing our faith. The carols are theological statements describing God's presence in the world. "The theology we sing," Sheri Kling asserts, "is also the theology we maintain in our hearts. We need to be astute in singing our hymns." Influenced by the relational and incarnational spirit of process theology, which sees God's presence everywhere and in all persons, Sheri has written several theologically inspired Christmas carols "that connect the traditional with the contemporary." Sheri, Daryl, and I agree that the carols we sing must witness to our commitment to unity and to the affirmation of contemporary voices. Liberated by song, we discover God's incarnation in every nation, culture, and race, and, most important, in our own lives as well as the lives of strangers we'll never meet.

Writing This Book

This is an especially personal book. As personal as any of the theological and spiritual texts I have penned, this book came from the heart and reflects my faith as a follower of the Bethlehem Child and Galilean mystic, healer, and prophet.

Several years ago, I initiated a spiritual practice that has transformed my life during Christmas and throughout the year. I began to truly live the twelve days of Christmas each year by devoting myself throughout the Christmas season to deepening my sense of Incarnation. I did this through a process of companioning with a particular spiritual guide, as well as the Christmas stories from Matthew, Luke, and John. I began each day by reading verses from scripture describing the birth of Jesus, along with passages from a particular author or stream of Christianity. Then I took my readings out for a walk in the quiet of the Cape Cod beach near our home and then, after a post-retirement move, in the suburban DC neighborhood where we now reside, letting my mind be filled with images of Jesus' birth, inspired by spiritual texts. I returned home and jotted down my insights, which eventually came to fruition in the twelve days of Christmas books. This book is the fifth in that series.[3]

This particular "twelve-days" text emerged from my daily focus on what is traditionally known as lessons and carols, reading a passage from scripture and then coupling that passage with a carol. I started each day by listening to several versions of each Christmas hymn, ranging from classical to popular, Eugene Ormandy and the Philadelphia Orchestra to Pentatonix, Brian Wilson, George Winston, Josh Groban, Perry Como, and Neil Diamond. I bathed my memories in the Goodyear Tires' *Great Songs of Christmas* and the carols I first heard on my parent's turntable in 1961 as a nine-year-old. I sang as I walked, allowing the emotions and images of Christmas to fill my spirit, and then, back home with a cup of coffee, I let the words flow on my computer screen. Often, I felt the words coming to me intuitively, emerging from my unconscious where God's Spirit speaks in "sighs too deep for words."

In the spirit of Mary Oliver, I noticed, was amazed, and wrote about it.

In many ways, this text, and its four predecessors, reflect the wisdom of Henry van Dyke, the lyricist of "Joyful, Joyful, We Adore Thee" and the author of the Christmas classic *The Story of the Other Wiseman:* "I would tell the tale as I heard fragments of it in the Hall of Dreams, in the palace of the Heart of [Humanity]."[4] Van Dyke's Hall and Heart are my Christmas memories: a boy growing up in the Salinas Valley, California; my mother taking us to the "land of sweets" with a once-a-year box of See's candies; listening to carols on vinyl; colored lights and the aroma of pine; going caroling through our neighborhood; and feeling that somehow Jesus walked with me, both the Baby and the resurrected Savior, who, as the hymn says, "told me that I was his own."

Reading This Book

As a voracious reader, I have found many ways to read any book, whether it is spiritual, devotional, theological, mystery, or historical. One way to experience this text is to couple your daily readings with listening to Christmas carols, either as a prelude or call to prayer or in the background. In a similar fashion, Daryl Hollinger describes his own Christmas practice: "I read the lyrics, meditate on them in the spirit of Lectio Divina,[5] or Holy Reading, and reflect on specific passages as a way of discovering its meaning for me."

I invite you to follow my own approach as I wrote this book and take a few minutes each of the days from December 25 to January 6 to listen to the carol suggested for that particular day. Let the music of Bethlehem guide your steps and inspire your actions. Then, in the spirit of Lectio Divina—holy reading—take time to pause, noticing the words that stand out; repeat and meditate on a particular word or phrase; and then ask God to reveal the meaning of these words for your life. Going deeper into the words and music, you join heart, mind, and hands, allowing Christmas to be the lens through which you see the world around you and everyone you meet. If you open to God's breath of life, the light of the world illumines you. In the words of Sheri Kling:

> *Breath of life in God's word animating us all.*
> *Sound and silence were heard, in Creation you called.*
> *You moved over the waters, in darkness gave birth*
> *To creative new forms that gave rise to the Earth,*
> *Penetrating each life with your bountiful worth.*
> *Spirit God, breathe anew in us all.*

Day 1
CHRISTMAS DAY

JOY TO THE WORLD

Joy to the world, the Lord is come!
Let Earth receive her King.
Let every heart prepare Him room
And heaven and nature sing,
And heaven and nature sing,
And heaven and heaven and nature sing.

But the angel said to the shepherds,
"Do not be afraid. I bring you good news
that will cause great joy for all the people.
Today in the town of David a
Savior has been born to you;
he is the Messiah, the Lord.

(Luke 2:10–11)

Joy to the world, our God is come. When British pastor and hymn-writer Isaac Watts (1674–1748) penned the words of "Joy to World" in 1719 as a hymn in his collection *The Psalms of David: Imitated in the Language of the New Testament*, he intended the hymn to be a celebration of Christ's victory over the powers of evil and his enthronement as Ruler of All Creation. Watts believed Christ would return to Earth to once and for all establish a commonwealth of justice and peace, healing our broken and wayward world. Inspired by Psalm 98, Watts saw the transformation of the world as embracing the human and nonhuman world.

> *Sing to God a new song,*
> *For God has done marvelous things. . . .*
> *All the ends of the earth have seen*
> *the salvation of our God.*
> (Psalm 98:1, 3)

Christmas is about joy! It is about good news for all people. Everything changes at Christmas. Our past, present, and future are flooded with God's radiant light. Christmas transforms our hearts and changes the way we look at the world and ourselves. The song of Mary—the Magnificat—is realized in time and space: the poor and weak rejoice at the bounty of God's new world order, and the wealthy no longer hoard power and possession (Luke 1:46–55). Our endings, even the hoped-for victory of the moral and spiritual arcs of history, are hidden in our beginnings, the birth of a Child. The Incarnation reveals God's love for the world, revealed in God's solidarity with all Creation and the power of God's love calling us to be love-givers, love-seekers, and love-finders in our personal lives, as well as our national and planetary citizenship.

The spiritual DNA of the universe is revealed in the Incarnation of Jesus in Bethlehem, and also in the first flash of the Big Bang nearly 14 billion years ago. During the Christmas season, we celebrate the wonders of God's love in the life of a little Baby, the children of our world, and the birthing room of the universe. Christmas reminds us that God is not neutral in the human and cosmic adventures. The philosopher Alfred North Whitehead (1861–1948) asserted that the aim of the universe is the production of beauty and growth. The Hubble and Webb telescopes witness to a beautiful God who brings forth a beautiful Creation of galaxies, planets, supernovas, and us. God has a vision and wants us to be part of it!

With beauty all around us, we walk; so rejoice the Navajo singers. The wonders of God's love reveal themselves in our cells and souls, and in the persistent aim at justice, the moral arc of the universe, invoked by both Unitarian Universalist minister Theodore Parker and Martin Luther King Jr.

God has a vision for you and our planet, and it is all about joy. All Creation repeats the sounding joy of a humble birth in Bethlehem, and heaven and Nature sing. "Joy to the world, the Lord is come." The joy of Jesus is coming to us right now. Jesus is being born in our world right now as the growing light that gives us hope as the nations "prove the glories of his righteousness" and "wonders of his love." We don't have to wait for a Second Coming to witness Christ's healing birth in our world: open your senses and spirit, for God is here right now, coming to us in the birth of the Holy Child and the face of every newborn baby.

CHRISTMAS QUESTIONS

Please take time to pause for prayerful contemplation. Then, as you listen to a version of "Joy to the World," consider these questions:

What gives you joy?

What would it mean for you to truly sing, "Joy to the world, our God is come"?

Where do you see Christ in the world today?

How can you be an apostle of joy?

A CHRISTMAS PRAYER

O Joyful God, thank you for Mary's little boy child, Jesus Christ. Thank you for the joy that created the galaxies, sun, moon, Earth, and me. Thank you for the joy deep down in my heart. Let my joy come forth in words of love and praise, and in hands to help and arms to hug. Amen.

Day 2

OF THE FATHER'S LOVE BEGOTTEN

Of the Father's love begotten,
Ere the worlds began to be,
He is Alpha and Omega,
He the source, the ending He,
Of the things that are, that have been,
And that future years shall see,
Evermore and evermore!

The angel said to her, "Do not be afraid, Mary, for you have found favor with God.

And now, you will conceive in your womb
and bear a son, and you
will name him Jesus.
He will be great and will be called
the Son of the Most High
and the Lord God will give to him
the throne of his ancestor David.

(Luke 1:30–32)

"Of the Father's Love Begotten" describes the original blessing of Divine Creation. The Incarnation is both cosmic and historical. In the birth of Jesus, the Infinite and finite meet, and eternity and time dance in joyful adoration. The Creative Word of God is embodied in human life, and the whole Earth is full of God's glory. Long before the emergence of human sin, before Jesus faced the Cross on Calvary, God brought forth a universe of beauty, order, and creativity. As Genesis affirms, when God created the world, God proclaimed that "it was good." Human life, in all its wonder, diversity, and ambiguity, was created "very good" (Genesis 1:1–31). Even the tragedies of life can be portals to experiencing beauty for those who awaken to God's presence in their lives and the world.

Theologians Bonaventure (1217–1274) and Nicholas of Cusa (1401–1464) both described God as being a circle, or sphere, "whose center is everywhere and whose circumference is nowhere." Bethlehem is the center of the universe. The Christ Child centers all things, and we are each at the center of God's love. Just as significant, the circumference, the outside of God's love, is nowhere and nonexistent. God loves all Creation without exception. The Birth in Bethlehem radiates across the universe, bringing joy and salvation to cells and galaxies, to amoebas and whales, to you and me. No one is lost, nobody is forsaken, and everyone eventually finds their way home— where they have been all along!

The angel announces glorious and world-transforming news to Mary of Nazareth. Mary's womb will be a "thin place," transparent to Divinity. The manger is a cathedral of love where the Cosmic Vision of the Holy Trinity meets the finite realities of human life. Mary gives birth to the Holy Child as God's gift of love to each of us. God loves us because of who we are, not in spite of who some people think we are or what we may think of ourselves—moral failures and depraved sinners, undeserving of love. God's aim is to love and heal us, never to punish us. That is the Gospel of Incarnation. To the dismay of the moral and religious police, even those we condemn as sinners—and the politicians we love to hate—are in the center of God's love.

The author of today's carol, lawyer and politician Aurelius Prudentius (348–413), spent his life on the Iberian Peninsula, today's Spain and Portugal. "Of the Father's Love Begotten" was penned when Prudentius turned to philosophy and poetry in later life. Music historians believe the poem was joined with plainsong (or chant) by the tenth century as a way of expressing the dynamic and creative nature of the Holy Trinity, and in particular the Son of God, Jesus the Christ.

God's love is still being born in our lives. You are created by love, and love is your destiny, as a child of the Alpha and Omega. You bear the face of God! You are loved!

CHRISTMAS QUESTIONS

Please take time to pause for prayerful contemplation. Then, as you listen to a version of "Of the Father's Love Begotten," consider the following questions:

Where do you see the Christ Child born in our world?

Where do you see the Christ Child being born in your life?

How might you become a midwife of God's Incarnation in the world?

A CHRISTMAS PRAYER

Creative God, whose center is everywhere and whose circumference is nowhere, help me be centered in your infinite and personal love. Let your wondrous love flow through me to all Creation, bringing joy to the world. Amen.

Day 3

IN THE
BLEAK WINTER

In the bleak midwinter,
frosty wind made moan.
Earth stood hard as iron, water like a stone.
Snow had fallen,
snow on snow, snow on snow,
In the bleak midwinter, long ago.

Now the birth of Jesus
the Messiah took
place in this way.
When his mother
Mary had been
engaged to
Joseph, but
before they lived
together,
she was found
to be pregnant
from the Holy Spirit.

Her husband Joseph, being a righteous man and unwilling to expose her to public disgrace, planned to divorce her quietly. But just when he had resolved to do this, an angel of the Lord appeared to him in a dream and said, "Joseph, son of David, do not be afraid to take Mary as your wife, for the child conceived in her is from the Holy Spirit. She will bear a son, and you are to name him Jesus, for he will save his people from their sins."

(Matthew 1:18–21)

Joseph is a dreamer, like his namesake from the Hebrew scripture, the one of "the amazing technicolor dream coat." Joseph of Nazareth doesn't cultivate dreams or anticipate revelations. They simply come to him at pivotal moments of his life.

Ancient spiritual guides, predecessors to today's Jungian dream interpreters, believed God communicated to humankind through dreams. The Hebrew patriarch Jacob dreams of a ladder of angels, receives a blessing, and stammers, "God was in this place, and I did not know it" (Genesis 28:16). Jacob's youngest child Joseph regularly receives dreams that reveal the significance of contemporary events and give guidance in relation to the future.

In one of the most significant passages in scripture, Joseph the Nazareth, a carpenter by trade, ponders what to do in his relationship with Mary, to whom he is betrothed. She is pregnant, and he isn't the father! He wants to ensure her well-being, but he is unsure about marrying her. An angel visits him in a dream and counsels him to go through with the marriage. Later, Joseph receives dreams that alert him to flee to Egypt to escape Herod's wrath and then to return to Nazareth after the death of Herod. Like Mary, Joseph receives the angelic affirmation, "Do not be afraid." Like his bride-to-be, Joseph also embraces the impossible possibility. He says "yes" to a future he doesn't fully understand, trusting God to provide a way forward where he perceives no way ahead.

"In the Bleak Midwinter" is based on a poem by an English poet, the child of an Italian political exile, Christina Rossetti (1830–1894). The poem was published, under the title "A Christmas Carol," in the January 1872 issue of *Scribner's Monthly,* and was first collected in the poet's collection *Goblin Market, The Prince's Progress and Other Poems.* Gustav Holst, composer of "The Planets," set Rossetti's poem to music. Together, Holst and Rosetti witnessed to light that pierces the darkness and shows us a pathway to the future. Even in the depth of winter, our hearts can be strangely warmed by God's ever-incarnating love.

After safely returning his family to Nazareth, Joseph is no longer mentioned in scripture. His absence has led readers to wonder whether he died sometime during the "lost years" between Jesus' Temple appearance at twelve and the beginning of Jesus' ministry at thirty. Although we do not know his entire story, the faithful Joseph is a model for our own spiritual adventures. At a pivotal moment, he says "yes" to God's vision of salvation, and his "yes" invites us to experience God's call in our dreams and synchronous encounters. When we are open to Divine wisdom, even bleak winter can reveal the interplay of God's love and our faithful response:

> *What can I give Him,*
> *Poor as I am?*
> *If I were a Shepherd,*
> *I would bring a lamb;*
> *If I were a Wise Man,*
> *I would do my part,*
> *Yet what I can I give Him—*
> *Give my heart.*

CHRISTMAS QUESTIONS

Please take time to pause for prayerful contemplation. Then, as you listen to a version of "In the Bleak Midwinter," consider the following questions:

Has your life ever been transformed by a dream?

In what synchronous and unexpected ways have you received God's guidance?

What visions draw you forward today?

What would it mean for you to "give your heart" to the Christ Child?

A CHRISTMAS PRAYER

Heart of the Universe, I give you my heart.
Help me to share what is most precious to me
with both my loved ones
and the "least of these" you spoke of in the Gospel.
Give me a heart of praise, thanksgiving, and compassion,
serving you as I care for the world around me. Amen.

Day 4

GOOD CHRISTIAN FRIENDS REJOICE

Good Christian friends, rejoice
with heart and soul and voice;
give ye heed to what we say:
News, news!
Jesus Christ is born today!
Ox and ass before him bow,
and he is in the manger now.
Christ is born today!

"She will bear a son,
and you are to name him Jesus,
for he will save his people from their sins."
All this took place to fulfill
what had been spoken
by the Lord through the prophet:
'Look, the virgin shall become pregnant
and give birth to a son, and they
shall name him Emmanuel,'
which means, 'God is with us.'"
When Joseph awoke from sleep,
he did as the angel of the
Lord commanded him;
he took her as his wife.

(Matthew 1:21–25)

In reflecting on the grace of God, which transforms our lives and gives us peace in times of conflict, the apostle Paul asserts, "Rejoice in God always; again, I will say, Rejoice!" (Philippians 4:4). This same joy is the heart of the Christmas season. "Joy to the world, the Lord is come," we carol. Christ is here and born to save.

Christmas is not intended to be an anthropocentric holiday. The Word that becomes flesh also gives birth to all

Creation (John 1:1–5, 9). "Ox and ass before Christ bow." The Incarnation changes humankind and transforms the nonhuman world. Animals, plants, soil, and stones—all are part of God's economy of love, and everything that breathes praises God. What begins with a hymn calling humankind to joy and thanksgiving resounds across all Creation. The whole world is in God's hands, and God's hands are loving. On Christmas, bells and birds cry out. Wolves howl and humpbacked whales sing.

Everything embodied is worthy of reverence because of Bethlehem's stable, and it deserves our ethical affirmation. In these precarious times of global climate change, "we need a little Christmas," in which we live more simply, making donations to programs like Heifer Project, Environmental Defense Fund, and Greenpeace, not to mention programs that support refugees and houseless people. In doing so, we honor the Child of all Creation. Dreaming of Christmases to come, we may choose, as Mother Elizabeth Seton counseled, to "live simply so that others might simply live."[6]

The origins of "Good Christian Friends Rejoice" are unclear. Michael Hawn, professor of Church Music at Perkins School of Theology, notes that the hymn may date from the fourth century. Other scholars attribute it to fourteenth-century German mystic Henry Suso. Anglican priest and hymn-writer John Mason Neale (1818–1866) translated it from Greek and Latin.[7]

Let us rejoice in Christ's birth! Let us sing songs of celebration and liberation, "high as the list'ning skies" and "loud as the rolling sea."[8] Eternal bliss is ours, and we share that bliss with all Creation. Christ is born to save, yes, Christ is born to save us and all Creation.

CHRISTMAS QUESTIONS

Please take time to pause for prayerful contemplation. Then, as you listen to a version of "Good Christian Friends Rejoice," consider the following questions:

What was your greatest joy as a child?

Do you ever experience that same joy now?

The Flying Scot Eric Liddell, whose balance of faith and athletics is portrayed in *Chariots of Fire*, asserted, "God made me fast, and when I run, I feel God's pleasure."

What gifts has God given you that bring out your joy and your experience of God's pleasure?

How might you express your reverence for the nonhuman world?

A CHRISTMAS PRAYER

*God of celebration and joy,
enliven and enlighten the childlike joy in me.
Let your joy fill my life,
radiating to the heavens and descending to the depths.
Let my joy inspire compassion and action
on behalf of our troubled planet, bringing joy
to human and nonhuman alike. Amen.*

Day 5

ONCE IN ROYAL DAVID'S CITY

Once in royal David's city
Stood a lowly cattle shed
Where a mother laid her baby
In a manger for His bed.
Mary was that mother mild,
Jesus Christ her little child. . . .
For He is our childhood's pattern.
Day by day like us He grew.

He was little, weak, and helpless,
Tears and smiles like us He knew,
And He feeleth for our sadness,
And He shareth in our gladness.

In those days a decree went out from
Caesar Augustus that all the world
should be registered. This was the
first registration and was taken while
Quirinius was governor of Syria. All
went to their own towns to be registered.
Joseph also went from the town of
Nazareth in Galilee to Judea, to the city
of David called Bethlehem, because
he was descended from the house and
family of David. He went to be registered
with Mary, to whom he was engaged
and who was expecting a child.

(Luke 2:1–5)

Each year I wait expectantly to view the Christmas Eve
Service of Lessons and Carols held in the chapel at Kings
College. In the darkness of the sanctuary, a lone child's voice

calls out "Once in Royal David's city," to be joined in the second and following stanzas by an ever-expanding circle of carolers, culminating in congregational song.

One voice can drown out the shouts of hatred. One light can cast out the gloom of fear. One Child can change everything and inspire a world of praise. The Child of Bethlehem and the birth of our child or grandchild, nephew, or niece will change the world forever. The small cry of the Bethlehem Child reverberates across the planet, bringing hope and healing to struggling humankind and the nonhuman world as well.

While we may not agree with the outmoded concept of a three-story universe depicted in the words, "He came down to earth from heaven," invoked in the hymn, we can affirm that something unique and special occurred in Bethlehem's stable. Unimaginative literalism and suspicious liberalism cannot snuff out the mysterious and marvelous stable light. The Creator of the Universe, the Divinity-Ever-Active-and-Always-Loving, moves in the concreteness and limitation of a Jewish child and his parents, and brings forth new life in our own daily struggles.

The philosopher Alfred North Whitehead described God as "the fellow sufferer who understands." I would add that God is the intimate Companion who celebrates. The

One "who comes down from heaven" is one of us. He is our childhood's pattern / Day by day like us He grew. . . . And He feeleth for our sadness / And He shareth in our gladness."

Jesus "grew in wisdom and stature and favor with God and humankind" (Luke 2:52). Listen again: *"Jesus grew."* His wisdom, empathy, and compassion expanded with growing awareness of his vocation as God's Beloved Child in solidarity with all humankind. Jesus is "our childhood's pattern," whether we are five, ten, twelve, forty, or in our seventies like me. Christ becomes one of us, so that we can become Christlike. This is the meaning of the ancient Christian vision of human destiny: *theosis* or divinization. In God's eyes, we are not abject sinners, undeserving of love. We are beloved children on our way to realizing our full humanity, fully alive and fully loving, unique expressions of God's glory.

Perhaps, the vision of what we may become was the inspiration of Anglo-Irish hymn-writer and poet Cecil Francis Alexander (1818–1895). Alexander penned "Once in Royal David's City" and "All Things Bright and Beautiful" as ways to share God's love with children. The Child in Bethlehem's stable comes to every child, reflecting their culture and their ethnic pigment, calling forth their unique and beautiful gifts. If our children begin life realizing that God loves them, their lives matter, and they—like baby

Jesus—can grow to do great things for God and the world, they are on their way to living joyful and meaningful lives of service and compassion.

As we contemplate "Once in Royal David's City," let us bring out the joyful and liberated child in ourselves and commit ourselves to creating a world where all children can realize their full potential as God's beloved, fully human, fully alive, fully loved and loving.

CHRISTMAS QUESTIONS

Please take time to pause for prayerful contemplation. Then, as you listen to a version of "Once in Royal David's City," consider the following questions:

How do you imagine Jesus' birth in the Bethlehem stable?

How do you experience Christ as your intimate companion in joy and sorrow?

When did you last let the Christmas child in you come out to play?

Where is God calling you to support the children in your life, community, and planet?

A CHRISTMAS PRAYER

In a lowly stable, you come to us, O Jesus.
On the borderlands of the United States,
you shiver in the cold, dear Christ Child.
In every haunt of poverty and loneliness, you dwell.
Open my heart that I might see your face,
in the lonely, in immigrants and forgotten elders,
and in the mirror.
Open my hands to share love and challenge injustice,
inspired by your love that "feeleth for our sadness
And . . . shareth in our gladness." Amen.

O LITTLE TOWN
OF BETHLEHEM

O little town of Bethlehem
How still we see thee lie
Above thy deep and dreamless sleep
The silent stars go by
Yet in thy dark streets shineth
The everlasting light
The hopes and fears of all the years
Are met in thee tonight.

While they were there,
the time came for her to deliver her child.
And she gave birth to her firstborn son
and wrapped him in bands of cloth
and laid him in a manger,
because there was no place
in the guest room.

(Luke 2:6–7)

Virtually every morning before sunrise, I head out on a three-mile trek through my Potomac, Maryland, neighborhood. Just a handful of miles from the White House, Capitol, and Supreme Court, our suburban community is silent as I hit the trail. Only a stray cat, fox, and family of deer are my companions as I quietly walk the dark streets of suburban Washington, DC. Some mornings, I spend my walk in prayer and meditation, or in reflection on what I hope to write when I return home. Other mornings, my heart is troubled, and my mind is churning with thoughts of conflict and catastrophe.

We have our own would-be Caesars and despots in the twenty-first century: prevaricating politicians, white nationalists, hate-filled religious leaders, ruthless moguls, whose self-interest and lust for power and control stifles world loyalty and care for the ones Jesus called "the least of these." Although the world is still and the "silent stars go by," I am not at peace. I know what it means to confess, "the hopes and fears of all the years are met in thee tonight" as I ruminate about our inability—and lack of desire—to respond to the reality of climate change and to heal the wounded soul of our nation. In moments like these, the words of today's carol calm and comfort my soul.

The text of this hymn was written by Phillips Brooks (1835–1893), Episcopal priest and rector of Church of the Holy Trinity, Philadelphia, and later of Trinity Church, Boston. He was inspired by his visit to the village of Bethlehem in 1865; three years later, he wrote the poem for his church. As Christmas approached, Brooks told the organist at the Church of the Holy Trinity, Lewis Redner (1831–1908), that he needed music for the poem by Sunday morning; Redner rushed to accommodate the request.

"On the Saturday night previous my brain was all confused about the tune," Redner wrote. "I thought more about my Sunday-school lesson than I did about the music. But I was roused from sleep late in the night hearing an angel-strain whispering in my ear, and seizing a piece of music paper I jotted down the treble of the tune as we now have it, and on Sunday morning before going to church I filled in the harmony." Redner confessed that neither he nor Phillips Brooks thought the carol would live beyond that Christmas of 1868, and yet it has taken on a life of its own, inspiring persons each Christmas season.[9]

"O Little Town of Bethlehem" concludes with a prayer for God's incarnation to become real in our own lives. As I read these lyrics, I am once again the nine-year-old who dreamed of peace on Earth, goodwill to all, as he listened to the Goodyear Tire's *Great Songs of Christmas* album.

> *O holy Child of Bethlehem*
> *Descend to us, we pray*
> *Cast out our sin and enter in*
> *Be born in us today*
> *We hear the Christmas angels*
> *The great glad tidings tell*
> *Oh, come to us, abide with us*
> *Our Lord Immanuel!*

In these challenging personal and global times, we need to experience God's presence in our lives. We need God's companionship to guide us toward a peaceful and just future.

CHRISTMAS QUESTIONS

Please take time to pause for prayerful contemplation. Then, as you listen to a version of "O Little Town of Bethlehem," consider the following questions:

What are your "hopes and fears" for yourself,
loved ones, community, nation, and planet?

Where do you see Christ's presence
in the challenges you face?

What would it be like for Christ to abide with you?

How would it change your life?

A CHRISTMAS PRAYER

Oh Holy Child of Bethlehem, be born in us today,
enter into our lives, and abide with us.
Give us hope and the courage to live out your dream
for our lives and this good Earth. Amen.

SILENT NIGHT

Silent night, holy night,
all is calm, all is bright
round yon virgin
mother and child.
Holy infant, so
tender and mild,
sleep in
heavenly peace,
sleep in
heavenly peace.

Now in that same region
there were shepherds living in the fields,
keeping watch over their flock by night.
Then an angel of the Lord
stood before them,
and the glory of the Lord
shone around them,

and they were terrified.
But the angel said to them,
"Do not be afraid, for see,
I am bringing you good news of great joy
for all the people.

(Luke 2:8–10)

In the fierce fighting of the Battle of the Bulge in December 1944, as the German leaders began one last attempt to save their nation from defeat, a mother and her young son entertained seven guests: four German and three American soldiers.

Fritz Vincken and his mother had been sent by Fritz's father to live in a forest cabin to escape the ravages of war. It was Christmas Eve, and Fritz and his mother were prepared to celebrate with a simple meal, when there was a knock on the door. Fritz's mother opened the door to two American soldiers, carrying a wounded comrade. She put them to work preparing the Christmas meal, now expanded with the unexpected company.

Another knock came, and four German soldiers appeared on their doorstep, separated from their comrades, shivering in the cold December night and asking for shelter. To their request, Fritz's mother replied, "Of course, you can also have a fine, warm meal and eat till the pot is empty. . . . But," she added firmly, "we have three other guests, whom you may not consider friends. . . . This is Christmas Eve, and there will be no shooting here."

Fritz's mother continued, "You could be my sons, and so could they in there. A boy with a gunshot wound, fighting for his life, and his two friends, lost like you and just as hungry and exhausted as you are. This one night," she turned to the corporal and raised her voice a little, "this Christmas night, let us forget about killing."

The two groups of soldiers put down their guns, ate together, and then one of the German soldiers, who had studied medicine, provided medical care to the wounded Americans. As they departed the next day, the German soldiers alerted the American soldiers to dangers on their return path to their battalion.

As a final blessing, Fritz's mother said to the now-armed soldiers, "Be careful, boys. I want you to get home someday where you belong. God bless you all!" The German and American soldiers shook hands, and Fritz and his mother watched them disappear in opposite directions.

Then she opened her Bible to Matthew 12:21: "They departed their country another way." Their visit had been an unexpected blessing, giving the soldiers a heavenly peace for which we all yearn.[10] Today's carol, "Silent Night," expresses well that state of celestial stillness.

"Stille Nacht" was first performed on Christmas Eve 1818 at St. Nicholas parish church in Oberndorf, in present-day Austria. Two years before, the village priest Joseph Mohr (1799–1848) had written the poem in the wake of the Napoleonic Wars. On Christmas Eve 1818, Mohr brought the words to Franz Gruber (1787–1863), schoolmaster and organist in the nearby village of Arnsdorf, and asked him to compose a melody. The music needed to be suited for a guitar accompaniment for that night's mass, since flooding had damaged the church organ. Out of necessity, emerged beautiful music. Out of scarcity, rose abundance. In all things, God works for goodness, truth, and beauty.

We need to go home by another way. We need an alternative to greed, incivility, violence, and injustice. We need to practice peace on Earth, that heavenly peace, that comes from going home by another way.

CHRISTMAS QUESTIONS

Please take time to pause for prayerful contemplation. Then, as you listen to a version of "Silent Night," consider the following questions:

Where do you find stillness and heavenly peace?

Where is God leading you to be an "instrument of peace"?

What new pathways do you need to take to be a peacemaker in your family, community, and nation?

A CHRISTMAS PRAYER

Loving God, let your peace descend on me.
Make me an instrument of your peace.
Let my life bring people together in the Christmas Spirit
of peace on Earth, goodwill to all.
Let me seek to find ways
to overcome my own alienation from others.
Out of my own healing,
may I bring healing to this good Earth. Amen.

Day 8

NEW YEAR'S DAY

ANGELS WE HAVE HEARD ON HIGH

Shepherds, why this jubilee?
Why your joyous strains prolong?
What the gladsome tidings be
Which inspire your heavenly song?

Gloria, in excelsis deo
Gloria, in excelsis deo.

Now in that same region there were shepherds living in the fields, keeping watch over their flock by night. Then an angel of the Lord stood before them, and the glory of the Lord shone around them, and they were terrified. But the angel said to them, "Do not be afraid, for see, I am bringing you good news of great joy for all the people: to you is born this day in the city of David a Savior, who is the Messiah, the Lord. This will be a sign for you: you will find a child wrapped in bands of cloth and lying in a manger." And suddenly there was with the angel a multitude of the heavenly host, praising God and saying,

> "Glory to God in the highest heaven,
> and on earth peace among
> those whom he favors!"

(Luke 2:8–14)

"**A**ngels We Have Heard on High" is always a vocal test for me. Each Christmas Eve, I challenge myself to make it all the way through the sixteen up-and-down notes of the "Gloria" without taking a breath. Most of the time I make it!

Encountering angels is always a test for humankind. The Christmas angels are not cuddly little cherubs; they are majestic messengers from God, coming in forms to which we mortals can relate, often asking us to do what we perceive to be impossible tasks. When you meet an angel, whether in the Jerusalem Temple as did Isaiah seven hundred years before Jesus' birth, or as you are going about your daily chores like Mary of Nazareth, you always receive a task that initially appears beyond your abilities. But, as the saying goes, "When God gives you a task, God always gives you the resources to complete it!" God always makes a way where we see no way forward, whether we are confused and overwhelmed like Joseph, or awestruck and astonished like the shepherds.

In describing the shepherds' encounter with the Christmas angels, mystic and theologian Howard Thurman reflected that "there must be always remaining in every [person]'s life some place for the singing of the angels—someplace for that which in itself is breathlessly beautiful and by an inherent prerogative throwing all the rest of life into a new and created relatedness. Something that gathers up into itself all the freshets of experience from drab and commonplace areas of living and glows in one bright light of penetrating beauty and meaning—and then passes.

The commonplace is shot through now with new glory—old burdens become lighter, deep and ancient wounds lose much of their old, old hurting. A crown is placed over our heads that for the rest of our lives, we are trying to grow tall enough to wear. Despite all the crassness of life, despite all the harshness of life, life is saved by the singing of angels."[11]

Like many hymns and carols, the origin of "Angels We Have Heard on High" is uncertain. In 129 CE, Pope Telesphorus mandated that the "Gloria," or "Angels Hymn," the precursor of today's challenging chorus, be sung at Christmas Eve masses. French legends relate that on Christmas Eve, shepherds would cry *Gloria in excelsis Deo,* "Glory to God in the Highest," from one field to another to celebrate the Christ Child's birth. James Chadwick, the Anglo-Irish Bishop of Hexham and Newcastle in northeast England, paraphrased the words of "Angels We Have Heard on High" from the French carol, "Les Anges dans nos campagnes."

As Thurman says, when we hear the angelic voices, our lives take on a glow. As we run to Bethlehem, our hearts, like the Grinch of Dr. Suess's story, grow three times in size, and we receive a vision of what we can be as Christmas persons. The vision can last into the New Year and our whole life long.

CHRISTMAS QUESTIONS

Please take time to pause for prayerful contemplation. Then, as you listen to a version of "Angels We Have Heard on High," consider the following questions:

Have you ever encountered an "angel"?
If so, what was the experience like?

What God-inspired angelic vision of yourself are you seeking to grow into?

What dreams inspire your journey in the year ahead?

A CHRISTMAS PRAYER

God in the Highest, help me to listen for angelic voices
and when I hear these voices,
let me run with joyful abandon to
the stable of Bethlehem.
Let me in the running discover
that the manger in Bethlehem is everywhere
and that in every encounter, a humble child is born
and an adult is trying to find their way.
Let me grow in heart and mind large enough
to embrace the angel in everyone I meet. Amen.

Day 9

O COME, ALL YE FAITHFUL

Sing, choirs of angels,
Sing in exultation,
Sing, all ye citizens of heaven above;
Glory to God
In the highest.
O come, let us adore Him,
O come, let us adore Him,
O come, let us adore Him,
Christ the Lord!

When the angels had left them and gone into heaven, the shepherds said to one another, "Let us go now to Bethlehem and see this thing that has taken place, which the Lord has made known to us." So they went with haste and found Mary and Joseph and the child lying in the manger. When they saw this, they made known what had been told them about this child, and all who heard it were amazed at what the shepherds told them, and Mary treasured all these words and pondered them in her heart. The shepherds returned, glorifying and praising God for all they had heard and seen, just as it had been told them.

(Luke 2:15–20)

The first Christmas came to the most surprising people: a young peasant girl, her working-class fiancé, shepherds in their fields shivering in bitter cold, and religious teachers from another religious tradition and ethnic background.

While we may have romantic images of the shepherds, their lives were similar to cowboys on the prairie: rough and tumble, houseless, away from their families, uneducated, poorly paid, and considered lower class. Like many "essential workers" today, they were necessary in the food and clothing chain, and yet they were marginalized, scorned, and looked down upon by the elite, erudite, and educated. Think about the "necessary" people we barely notice in our own world until we need them: custodians and cleaners, sanitation workers, truck drivers, farmworkers, and homecare aides. The first Christmas message comes to minimum-wage employees and not the wealthy and wise, not the priests, potentates, or professors. Regardless of your social class, race, ethnicity, age, health condition, occupation, sexual identity, or gender, the Christmas angels can come to you.

"O Come All Ye Faithful" (originally written in Latin as "Adeste Fideles") has been attributed to various authors, including the Franciscan theologian and spiritual guide Saint Bonaventure (1217–1274), English hymnist John Francis Wade (1711–1786), English organist and composer John Reading (1645–1692), King John IV of Portugal (1604–1656), and anonymous Cistercian monks. Regardless of the author, the invitation resounds through the ages—to pay attention to angelic visitations, delight in their singing, and then race to Bethlehem to adore the Christ Child.

We don't speak about adoration much in everyday conversation. The word "adore" seems archaic or perhaps too intimate for those who see God as distant and indescribable. The Bethlehem God is infinite and also intimate. The "word made flesh" is among us, as near as our next breath. The personal God loves us dearly, and in return we can worship and love the Christ Child and his Creation, putting the God of Bethlehem first in our lives. We can let go of decorum and simply adore and praise the Child who walks among us, inviting us to share in the Hallelujah chorus. We can, as theologian-song writer Sheri Kling reflects, join with shepherds and angels as:

They sang the news as loud as thunder,
God's own Son in manger lay.
Sent to fill all hearts with wonder, and
heal the world in every way.
Do not fear the angels say, Christ is born among you today. . . .
But in our hearts, the deepest mystery,
God's own Son reborn in you!
Do not fear the angels say, Christ is born within you today!

CHRISTMAS QUESTIONS

Please take time to pause for prayerful contemplation. Then, as you listen to a version of "O Come All Ye Faithful," consider the following questions:

What desires motivate you?

What is the primary focus—or foci—of your desires?

Could God be the source of some of your deepest desires?

How do you feel when you realize that God is as near to you as your next breath— and that God loves you dearly and without end?

A CHRISTMAS PRAYER

God of heaven, Earth, and angelic host,
I ask for a loving heart. Fill my days with praise.
Fill my relationships with love.
Let me love you in all things
and love all things in your love. Amen

I HEARD THE BELLS ON CHRISTMAS DAY

And in despair I bowed my head;
"There is no peace on earth," I said;
"For hate is strong,
And mocks the song
Of peace on earth, good-will to men!"
Then pealed the bells more loud and deep:
"God is not dead, nor doth He sleep;
The Wrong shall fail,
The Right prevail,
With peace on earth, good-will to men."

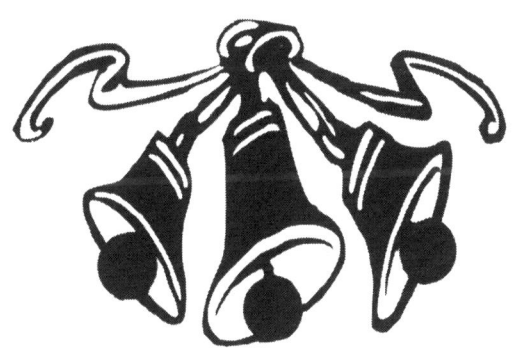

When Herod saw that he had
been tricked by the magi,
he was infuriated, and he sent
and killed all the children
in and around Bethlehem who
were two years old or under,
according to the time that he
had learned from the magi.

(Matthew 2:16)

There are days—even during the Christmas season—when I feel despair about what lies ahead. I worry about the future my grandchildren will inherit. I am anxious about our complacency despite the obvious signs our planet is in peril. Demagogic political leaders threaten the United States 'democracy. Nationalism, racism, and anti-Semitism are on the rise, much of it provoked by Christian communities. "There is no peace on earth, for hate is strong and mocks the song of peace on earth good will to all."

Life was much the same for Jesus and his parents. They lived in an oppressed country, never able to control their political destiny. Violence punctuated their days. Mary and Joseph fled, like millions of immigrants from Central America, South America, and Africa, to save their only child. As they sought asylum in Egypt, Herod unleashed the violent massacre of the children, seeking to kill every child in Bethlehem in his quest to eradicate the Christ Child. As if to demonstrate the ubiquity of violence against children throughout history, often perpetrated by governments, the Feast of the Holy Innocents is held, depending on locale, on several dates: December 27, 28, 29, and January 10.

Yet the bells of Christmas ring out. Despots and demagogues will eventually fall, remembered only for their evil. Hate will be quelled, revealed as fear in disguise. The children of slave owners and slaves will play together as a nation leans toward healing. The moral and spiritual arcs of history will outlast and outlive all the forces of evil.

American poet Henry Wadsworth Longfellow (1807–1882) wrote "I Heard the Bells on Christmas Day" during a time of personal and national anguish. In 1861, two years before writing this poem, Longfellow was devasted when his second wife was fatally burned in an accidental fire; Longfellow also suffered serious burns in the fire. Then, in 1863, Longfellow's oldest son, Charles, joined the Union Army without his father's blessing. Appointed as a lieutenant, he was severely wounded in early December at the Battle of Bull Run in Virginia. Longfellow wrote the poem on Christmas Day in 1863. The poet proclaimed the vision of peace on Earth and goodwill toward all in the context of the carnage of the Civil War.

Listen for the bells. Listen also for children crying and parents mourning. Listen for the voices of rage, and the soothing and healing of Jesus. Listen for whispers of hope and murmurs of possibility. Ring bells to proclaim your faith in God's future for you and the world, and your commitment to be God's companion in healing. The bells peal every day, announcing "God is not dead. Nor does God sleep."

CHRISTMAS QUESTIONS

Please take time to pause for prayerful contemplation. Then, as you listen to a version of "I Heard the Bells on Christmas Day," consider the following questions:

What most challenges your faith in the future?

Where do you most see the absence of God?

Where do you find the "the bells of Christmas" pealing with hope for the future?

Toward what actions is the moral and spiritual arc of the universe calling you?

A CHRISTMAS PRAYER

Be with me, Companion God,
in my hopelessness and despair.
Be with me in my complacency and apathy.
Let the bells peal in my life, awakening me to my role
in being a sign of hope for others,
for the lost, lonely, forgotten, and maligned.
Let every immigrant and impoverished
bear the face of Jesus and let me balance
national security with greater compassion.
Challenge me to loving activism as God's companion
in healing the Earth. Amen.

Day 11
O HOLY NIGHT

O Holy Night!
The stars are brightly shining.
It is the night of the dear Savior's birth!
Long lay the world in sin and error pining,
Till he appear'd and the soul felt its worth.
A thrill of hope, the weary soul rejoices
For yonder breaks a new
and glorious morn. . . .

Truly He taught us to love one another;
His law is love and His gospel is peace.
Chains shall He break for the
slave is our brother,
And in His name all oppression shall cease.
Sweet hymns of joy
in grateful chorus raise we,
Let all within us praise His holy name.

In the beginning was the Word,
and the Word was with God,
and the Word was God.
He was in the beginning with God.
All things came into being through him,
and without him not one
thing came into being.
What has come into being in him was life,
and the life was the light of all people.
The light shines in the darkness,
and the darkness did not overtake it.

(John 1:1–5)

*C*hristmas proclaims to all who listen that we live in a God-filled world. The seraphs chant to astonished Isaiah, "The whole earth is full of God's glory" (Isaiah 6:1–8), and the Gospel of John's prologue proclaims the universality of God's wisdom, creativity, and revelation. God's life and light are "the light of all people." And that means you! The Christmas Light that shone at the birth of the universe radiates through all Creation, through the stable in Bethlehem, and through every cell of your body. "Arise, shine, your light has come." (Isaiah 60:1)

John's prologue sadly notes that persons and institutions often prefer darkness over light and falsehood over truth (John 1:10–11).[12] This is evident in the rise of conspiracy theories, incivility, racism, military invasions, persecution of sexual minorities, and our ongoing preference for power over principle. Yet, the light of Bethlehem's star shines everywhere and on everyone, most especially on the lost and oppressed.

Many people believe we must become small for God to become big in our lives. John's prologue and "O Holy Night" proclaim the opposite. God's light enlightens everyone, John proclaims. The carol chants that in the birth of Jesus, "the soul felt its worth." Think big, love big, for God's vision for you is larger than you can ever imagine. As Irenaeus of Lyons (130–202), an early Christian priest-theologian, proclaimed, "The glory of God is a fully alive person."

"O Holy Night" (*Cantique de Noël*) was originally based on a French-language poem by poet Placide Cappeau. It was written in 1843 and set to music in 1847 by Adolphe Adam, to celebrate the renovation of the church organ in Roquemaure, France. Like many other carols, a political message is embedded in the lyrics, which led both to its popularity among those who sought to abolish slavery and to its omission in many congregations in America's South. In the spirit of Jesus' first message (Luke 4:18–19), the carol asserts: "Chains shall he break, for the slave is our brother, and in his name all oppression shall cease." The holiness of Christmas propels us to transform our world so that all children can grow to their full potential, as all adults delight in childlike adventures.

CHRISTMAS QUESTIONS

Please take time to pause for prayerful contemplation. Then, as you listen to a version of "O Holy Night," consider the following questions:

Where is God most present in your life?

Where do you need to become more fully alive?

What spiritual practices will help you claim your full potential as God's beloved child?

Where is God calling you to break the chains of oppression?

Where do you need to "arise and shine"?

A CHRISTMAS PRAYER

*Loving God, help me become fully alive
and fully attentive to the pain of others, near and far.
Transform my apathy to empathy
that I might be your companion
in breaking the chains of oppression. Amen.*

Day 12

THIS LITTLE LIGHT OF MINE

This little light of mine,
I'm gonna let it shine.
This little light of mine,
I'm gonna let it shine.
This little light of mine,
I'm gonna let it shine.
Let it shine, let it shine, let it shine.

Everywhere I go, I'm gonna let it shine.
Everywhere I go, I'm gonna let it shine.
Everywhere I go, I'm gonna let it shine.
Let it shine, let it shine, let it shine.

The true light, which enlightens everyone,
was coming into the world.

(John 1:9)

I n the darkest night, we see myriad stars. Growing plants need light, yet they germinate in the darkness of the soil. Jesus is the light of the world, and he grows in Mary's dark womb. John's Gospel contrasts darkness and light in spiritual and moral terms, distinguishing the children of darkness, who seek their own self-interest above God's realm, from the children of light, who recognize God's loving presence in Jesus and bring light to the world by their lives.

While I understand John's binary approach to spirituality, contrasting the children of light with the children of darkness, I prefer to use a continuum of self-interest to world loyalty, scarcity thinking to abundant living, greed to generosity, hate and fear to love and courage, apathy to empathy, to describe contrasting aspects of human experience. God's light reminds us that within every sinner there is a saint, and that every saint must humbly acknowledge their imperfections.

"You are the light of the world. . . . Let your light shine," Jesus proclaims. That is our calling: to see God's Christmas light, and then be God's light in the world.

The phrase "This little light of mine" first appeared in a 1925 poetry book by Edward G. Ivins. In 1933, newspapers provided the first known references to the song, reporting that a chorus sang it at an African Methodist Episcopal conference in Helena, Montana, from where Ivins hailed, and from there, it spread across the nation.

In her biography of civil rights activist Fannie Lou Hamer, Kay Mills notes, "If Mrs. Hamer had a theme song, it was 'This Little Light of Mine.'" Hamer believed in the power of song to transform persons and sustain protest. "Singing is one of the main things that can keep us going. When you're in a brick cell, locked up, and haven't done anything to anybody but still you're locked up there and sometimes words just begin to come to you, and you begin to sing. Like one of my favorite songs, 'This Little Light of Mine, I'm Going to Let it Shine.' This same song goes back to the fifth chapter of Matthew . . . where Jesus says a city that sets on a hill cannot be hid. Let your light shine so that [all people] would see your good works and glorify the father which is in heaven. I think singing is very important. It brings out the soul."

Recently, as I was walking at sunrise, I passed my oldest grandson's school, praying for him and his fellow students. A voice whispered in my ear, "Bruce, you are a knight of light. Be one!" That message has stayed with me throughout the Christmas season: to see the light where hate, fear, and dishonesty hide it; to recognize the light in those whom I oppose politically; to let the light of love and challenge shine and bring out the light of others. "This little light of mine, I'm gonna let it shine. . . . Everywhere I go, I'm gonna let it shine."

CHRISTMAS QUESTIONS

Please take time to pause for prayerful contemplation. Then, as you listen to a version of "This Little Light of Mine," consider the following questions:

Do you recognize that you are the "light of the world"?

What does this realization inspire in you?

What does it mean to let your light shine in your personal/relational, professional, and political life?

A CHRISTMAS PRAYER

*Light of the World, shine in and through me.
Awaken me to my identity as your "little light"
and help me to "let it shine, let it shine, let it shine . . .
everywhere I go." Amen.*

THE FEAST
OF EPIPHANY

GO TELL IT ON THE MOUNTAIN

Go, tell it on the mountain
Over the hills and everywhere
Go, tell it on the mountain
That Jesus Christ is born.

In the time of King Herod, after Jesus was born in Bethlehem of Judea, magi from the east came to Jerusalem, asking, "Where is the child who has been born king of the Jews? For we observed his star in the east and have come to pay him homage." When King Herod heard this, he was frightened, and all Jerusalem with him, and calling together all the chief priests and scribes of the people, he inquired of them where the Messiah was to be born. They told him, "In Bethlehem of Judea. . . .When they had heard the king, they set out, and there ahead of them, went the star that they had seen in the east, until it stopped over the place where the child was. When they saw that the star had stopped, they were overwhelmed with joy. On entering the house, they saw the child with Mary his mother, and they knelt down and paid him homage. Then, opening their treasure chests, they offered him gifts of gold, frankincense, and myrrh. And having been warned in a dream not to return to Herod, they left for their own country by another road.

(Matthew 2:1-5, 7–11)

The magi, followers of the faith of Zarathustra, follow a star to Bethlehem's stable. Foreigners, and adherents of another religious tradition, the magi discern what is hidden from Jerusalem's political and religious leaders. God speaks to the magi through a shining star, and then later in dreams, which alert them to bypass Herod and go home by another way.

God chose these three foreigners to share good news, while certain political and spiritual leaders of Jerusalem chose not to follow the revelation they were given. Once again, the Christmas stories tell us that there is another way. Epiphany continues the spirit of Christmas in its highlighting of God's ever-present grace that transcends nation, religion, age group, sexuality, and politics. We must shout the story of God's love on the mountaintop and the valley floor, the hospital room and the halls of Congress.

"Go Tell It on the Mountain" is an African-American spiritual, compiled by John Wesley Work Jr. (1871–1925), but dating back to at least 1865. As the director of the Fisk Jubilee Singers, an a cappella group still in existence, Work was responsible for taking the Singers on tour each year. He then served as president of Roger Williams University in Nashville, until his death in 1925. Working with his wife and his brother, Work collected slave songs and spirituals, publishing them as *New Jubilee Songs as Sung by the Fisk Jubilee Singers* (1901) and *New Jubilee Songs and Folk Songs of the American Negro* (1907), including the first publication of "Go Tell It on the Mountain," which he may have had a hand in composing.

This thirteenth day since Christmas Day, the Feast of Epiphany, is a day of celebration and (for some) gift-giving, reminding us that Christmas goes beyond the short liturgical season of twelve days. Incarnation is universal and personal and always fresh. The mercies of the Christ Child are new every morning, calling us to come to Bethlehem with magi and shepherds, to say "yes" to the angels with Mary, and to recognize the wisdom of dreams with Joseph. The carols and hymns of Christmas are still alive, regardless of our theology, because they tell our story of spiritual growth and companionship with God.

Let us go forth, knowing that the story of Jesus' birth is ever new and always fresh and constantly inspiring. Go tell it on the mountain that Jesus is Christ is born. Let us celebrate Christmas every day in the spirit of Howard Thurman's poem:

When the song of the angels is stilled,
when the star in the sky is gone,
when the kings and princes are home,
when the shepherds are back with their flocks,
the work of Christmas begins:
to find the lost,
to heal the broken,
to feed the hungry,
to release the prisoner,
to rebuild the nations,
to bring peace among the people,
to make music in the heart.[13]

CHRISTMAS QUESTIONS

Please take time to pause for prayerful contemplation. Then, as you listen to a version of "Go Tell It On the Mountain," consider the following questions:

How will you keep Christmas throughout the year?

What is your "work" of Christmas?

What message of Christmas will you tell on the mountains of your life?

A CHRISTMAS PRAYER

Help me, God of all people and places,
to shout your praises on the mountaintops.
Let my hallelujahs be full-throated.
Let my celebration of Christmas challenge me
to share the good news of peace on Earth,
goodwill to all. Amen.

NOTES

1. With Bruce Epperly, Daryl Hollinger is the author of *From a Mustard Seed: Enlivening Worship and Music in the Small Church* (Lanham, MD: Rowman and Littlefield, 2010).

2. Sheri Kling is the author of *A Process Spirituality: Christian and Transreligious Resources for Transformation* (Lanham, MD: Lexington Books, 2000).

3. The previous "twelve-day books" are: *The Work of Christmas: The Twelve Days of Christmas with Howard Thurman*, *I Wonder as I Wander: The Twelve Days of Christmas with Madeleine L'Engle*, *Thin Places Everywhere: The Twelve Days of Christmas with Celtic Christianity*, and *Repairing the World: The Twelve Days of Christmas with Francis and Clare of Assisi*.

4. Henry van Dyke, *The Story of the Other Wiseman* (Overland Park, KS: Digireads, 2004), 1.

5. Lectio Divina was developed in sixth-century monastic communities as a way of communicating with God through scripture. The four movements within Lectio Divina are reading, meditation, prayer, and contemplation. For a more detailed description, see https://mcgrathblog.nd.edu/how-to-practice-lectio-divina-praying-with-scripture.

6. Seton was the first North American canonized as a saint by the Roman Catholic Church.

7. Neale also translated "O Come, O Come, Emmanuel" and "Good King Wenceslas."

8. James Weldon Johnson (1871–1938), "Lift Every Voice and Sing." Johnson was a civil rights activist and a leader of the National Association for the Advancement of Colored People (NAACP).

9. In England and among Anglican and Episcopalian churches, the English folk ballad "Forest Green," collected and arranged by Ralph Vaughn, is the preferred melody.

10. The story is from Fritz Vincken, "Truce in the Forest," *Readers Digest* (January 1973), 111–114.

11. Howard Thurman, *The Mood of Christmas* (Richmond, IN: Friends United Press, 1985), 10–11.

12. The author of the Gospel of John relies on dark-and-light imagery. We need to remember, of course, that darkness need not equal evil, for darkness can also be fertile, womb-like; nor should we ever allow our cultural concept of negative darkness to affect how we think of people who have dark skin.

13. Thurman, 23.

More inspiration for
the Christmas season...

THE WORK OF CHRISTMAS
The 12 Days of Christmas
with Howard Thurman

This book is a celebration of the twelve days of Christmas, offering us a chance to dwell on the meaning of the season in dialogue with the wisdom of one of America's greatest mystics and activists, Howard Thurman.

During the twelve days of Christmas, our goal is to experience God's light, despite the temptation to close our hearts in a world too often characterized by racism, sexism, polarization, nationalism, and exclusion. This season asks us instead

to open our hearts and our lives, so that throughout the year ahead, we may be light-bearers, carrying the message of Divine justice and hope, making it come alive even in the darkest corners of the world. This is the year-round work of Christmas!

I WONDER AS I WANDER

The 12 Days of Christmas
with Madeleine L'Engle

How can we recover the radical meaning of the Christmas season? Using the thoughts and words of Madeleine L'Engle, this books offers you a guide through the hectic Christmas season. With quiet times of prayer, Scripture, and meditation, you can begin to wonder—to imagine big possibilities and ask important questions—as you wander outside your typical comfort zones. In the twelve days of Christmas, bookended by Christmas Eve and the Feast of Epiphany, you will experience anew the awe and wonder of the Incarnation.

As you both wonder and wander, the questions and images in this book will open your heart to the radical message of Christmas.

THIN PLACES EVERYWHERE
The 12 Days of Christmas
with Celtic Christianity

Bruce Epperly invites you to share a Christmas adventure with him, voyaging through the 12 days of Christmas (plus Christmas Eve and Epiphany) with Brendan, Columba, Brigid, Patrick, and other Celtic saints. With these Celtic adventurers as your companions, you will discover "thin places"—moments of time when the Incarnation of Christ shines through ordinary people, places, and events. After the busyness of Advent, the days that follow Christmas can be

a quieter time, when you can venture out on an inner vision quest for new ways of seeing and being.

May your Christmas journey awaken you to thin places everywhere.

REPAIRING THE WORLD
The 12 Days of Christmas with Francis & Clare of Assisi

During the Twelve Days of Christmas, Clare and her spiritual companion Francis ask us to consider the following questions:

- Where do I see Christ in my life and the world?

- What clutters my life, spiritually and physically?

- What one action can I take to simplify my life in order to protect the environment and promote the well-being of others?

In the lull after Christmas Day, join Bruce, Francis, and Clare on their quest to repair the world, taking you beyond presents and parties to world loyalty and holy restlessness.

SANTA CLAUS
Saint, Shaman, & Symbol

If you don't believe in Santa, you might want to reconsider. The familiar fellow dressed in red has been around a lot longer than the malls' Santa, longer than Rudolph, longer even than "The Night Before Christmas." His earliest and most ancient forms brought hope and cheer to generation after generation of humankind—and he still has a message for us today. In the midst of the materialism of the modern

holiday, Santa offers us a bridge between the physical, secular world and the spiritual, sacred realm. Discover his history and evolution, from Ice Age shaman to medieval saint to modern-day icon. Get to know Santa—and believe all over again.

Prepare the Way
Celtic Prayers for
the Season of Light

Ray Simpson has given his life, both professionally and personally, to Celtic Christianity, and now he helps us to celebrate a Celtic outlook on the season of Christmas. With their eloquent yet simple words, his prayers welcome the Holy One who comes to us in small, ordinary ways, who is present in the helpless and the vulnerable. As we join Ray in prayer, we stand on the threshold to paradox and mystery—and we "prepare the way" for God to enter our world anew.

RAY SIMPSON

Prepare the Way

Celtic Prayers for
the Season of Light

BRUCE G. EPPERLY has served as a seminary professor and administrator, university chaplain, and congregational pastor. An ordained minister with the United Church of Christ and Christian Church (Disciples of Christ), he is the author of more than sixty books, including *From Cosmos to Cradle: Meditations on the Incarnation* and *The Elephant is Running: Process and Open and Relational Theology and Religious Pluralism.*

ANACOCHARA
BOOKS

AnamcharaBooks.com

Made in the USA
Columbia, SC
26 November 2024

47635185R10069